GOMER

Ruel Fordyce

ISBN: 9798340254986

Dedication

To all the GOMER's seeking for real LOVE.

Contents

Acknowledgements

Special thanks to the closest people within my circle; my wife Nora, and sons Mathias and Santiago Fordyce, my dad Newburn Fordyce, my mom Jennifer Fordyce and my brother Rawle Fordyce and friends, who have helped and shaped my journey thus far.

The Crooked Symphony

In the beginning,
God whispers to the prophet,
and the words that fall from His lips
are not petals, but stones.
He tells Hosea,
"Go.
Find her.
The one the world will turn away from,
the one whose name will be a punchline
long before it's a prayer."

And Hosea,
his feet heavy as the burden he carries,
moves toward a love
he didn't ask for.
A love that stretches the seams of his skin,
makes a mockery of pride.
God says,
"Find Gomer,
the one who has wandered,

whose heart is a revolving door,
and make her your wife."

Imagine the look in Hosea's eyes—
a man standing at the intersection
of divine instruction and human heartbreak.
God doesn't promise ease,
but He promises purpose,
and in this crooked symphony,
He writes their names
on a score sheet of redemption.

Hosea finds her,
just as God said,
Gomer—
a woman broken in places no hand could reach.
A heart patched with the cloth of strangers,
a soul stitched together
by the threads of temporary comfort.
But still, Hosea looks at her
and sees the future
of a love that could change the course of history,
a reflection of a covenant
that would bleed for centuries.

He takes her hand,
softly, firmly,
as if to say,
"I see you,
not the rumors
that dance like smoke around your name,
not the echoes of past embraces
that have tried to claim you.

I see the you that God sees,
the one worthy of this impossible love."

And they wed,
not in a garden of roses
but in a wilderness of thorns,
a marriage inked in pain,
in promises that feel like they might break
under the weight of their own expectation.

She bears him children.
Each one named for a prophecy,
each one carrying the weight of a nation's rebellion:
Jezreel—God will scatter,
Lo-Ruhamah—no mercy,
Lo-Ammi—not my people.
Their names a mirror,
reflecting the cracks in a covenant
Israel had forgotten to cherish.

Still, Hosea stays.
Through the nights when Gomer's absence
hangs heavy in the air,
when her wandering spirit
pulls her into the arms of others.
Hosea's heart,
it stretches like a canvas,
takes in every brushstroke of pain,
and still he waits,
still he loves.

How can a man love a woman
who runs from him
like the sun runs from the night?

How can God love a people
who forget His name
in the silence of their prayers?

This is the question
Hosea's life answers,
a living parable,
a love story written
in the margins of Israel's rebellion.

And when Gomer returns,
eyes lowered,
cloaked in shame,
Hosea lifts her chin.
"I will buy you back,"
he says,
and in that moment,
he is not just a husband
but a savior,
not just a man
but a reflection of a God
whose love knows no limits,
whose forgiveness
is not a ledger
to be balanced,
but a well
to be drawn from endlessly.

Hosea's life,
his love for Gomer,
becomes the metaphor for us all—
for the times we have wandered,
for the days when our hearts
were more desert than garden,

for the nights when we sought refuge
in places that could never hold us.

And yet,
God stands at the door,
like Hosea,
waiting,
not with anger,
but with open arms,
whispering,
"I will buy you back."

Because love like this,
love that chases,
love that forgives before forgiveness is even asked,
love that stretches wide enough
to hold a world in rebellion,
that is the kind of love
God calls us to see.

Hosea may have been a prophet,
but in the end,
he was also a mirror—
reflecting a love
we can barely comprehend,
but that somehow
has been ours
from the very beginning.

A Love Song No More

In the echo of silence,
God speaks again,
and this time, His words fall like rain
onto the barren ground of a broken covenant.

Hosea, standing in the middle of his grief,
hears the voice of the Almighty
wrap around him like wind,
shaking him from the roots of his soul.
And this is what God says:
"Plead with your mother, plead—
for she is no longer my wife,
and I am no longer her husband."

This isn't a love song anymore.
This is a lament,
a dirge for a nation that once danced
in the arms of its Creator,

now stumbling in the dark,
chasing shadows that offer nothing but emptiness.

Israel has become like Gomer,
a bride who has forgotten
the vows she whispered beneath the stars,
who has traded promises for pleasures
that vanish like mist in the morning sun.

And God,
He is not silent.
He speaks of vines that will wither,
of walls that will fall.
He speaks of a land laid bare,
of treasures turned to dust,
because Israel has run after other lovers,
called them gods,
and forgotten the one who carved her name
into the palms of His hands.

"She said,
'I will go after my lovers,
who give me bread and water,
my wool and my flax,
my oil and my drink.'"
But what she doesn't know
is that the bread came from God's hands,
that the water was drawn from His well,
that every gift she thought was theirs to give
had been placed in her lap
by the One she now ignores.

How often do we become like Gomer?
Forgetting the One

who provides the breath in our lungs,
running to empty wells
with buckets full of hope,
only to return with nothing but regret.

But God,
He is both just and merciful,
both warrior and poet,
and this is the part of the story
where judgment gives way to redemption,
where wrath steps aside
so grace can speak.

He says,
"I will hedge up her way with thorns,
build a wall so she cannot find her paths.
She will chase her lovers but not overtake them.
She will seek them but not find them."
And when she is lost in the wilderness,
when every road leads her back to the emptiness
she tried to flee from,
God will be there.

Because love is not just an open hand.
Sometimes, love is a wall,
sometimes it is thorns,
sometimes it is every door closing
until the only way out
is the way back.

But then,
the shift.

God, in His infinite tenderness,
says,
"Therefore, behold, I will allure her,
bring her into the wilderness,
and speak tenderly to her."
And the desert,
the place of exile,
becomes a sanctuary,
a space for healing,
a place where the heart can hear
what it once drowned out in the noise of false
promises.

"I will give her vineyards from there,
and the Valley of Achor as a door of hope."
In the very place of trouble,
God will plant hope,
like a seed that pushes through the cracks of dry
ground,
like a song rising from the dust.

And Israel,
like Gomer,
will return.
She will call Him "My Husband"
and no longer "My Baal."
The names of false gods will be wiped from her lips,
and the sky will clear,
and the land will breathe again.

But this isn't just about a nation.
This is about us.
We are the ones who run,
who chase after the things that promise fulfillment

but leave us empty.
We are the ones who forget,
who need to be allured
back into the arms of the One
who loved us first,
who never stopped loving us
even when we turned our backs.

God says,
"I will betroth you to Me forever.
I will betroth you in righteousness and justice,
in steadfast love and mercy.
I will betroth you to Me in faithfulness,
and you shall know the Lord."

This is not just a promise.
This is a vow.
A covenant renewed,
a love restored,
a relationship made whole
not because we earned it,
but because God's love is the kind
that refuses to let go,
even when we run,
even when we fall.

And in that day,
the earth will respond—
the grain, the wine, the oil,
they will all rise up
to declare that love has won,
that mercy has triumphed
over judgment,
that we, the not-loved,

have become the beloved.
That we, the not-my-people,
have been called the children
of the living God.

Hosea's heart breaks open,
and in its cracks,
God plants the seeds of grace.
This is not just his story.
This is our story.
A love that chases,
a love that finds,
a love that redeems
even when we didn't know
we needed to be saved.

Soaked in Grief

The word of the Lord came again,
but this time it felt like a wound
wrapped in a whisper.
Hosea's heart was already heavy,
dragging behind him like a shadow,
and yet, God spoke—
not with rage, but with resolve.
And what He asked
wasn't something you find in love stories
or the romantic daydreams
of the hopeful.

"Go again,
love a woman who is loved by another man
and is an adulteress."
God's voice doesn't tremble,
it doesn't stutter,
it carves through the silence like a blade,
but this is not punishment,
this is poetry.

A love story soaked in grief
but forged in grace,
because God knows
that to love someone
who keeps leaving
is to understand the depth of forgiveness.

So, Hosea goes.
He goes,
not with the fire of righteous anger,
not with the fists of a man scorned,
but with the open palms
of someone who knows
that love, true love,
never runs out of second chances.
He finds her—
Gomer—
his wife and his wound,
in the marketplace,
standing on an auction block,
a price tag hanging from her wrists.
She is being sold,
her worth measured in silver,
her dignity stripped
in the open air
for all to see.

Hosea doesn't turn away,
doesn't look down at his feet.
He steps forward,
looks her in the eyes,
and he buys her back.
Fifteen shekels of silver
and a measure of barley—

that's what it cost to redeem
what was already his.
It doesn't seem like much
until you realize
that love always pays a higher price
than we expect.

He takes her hand,
gently, like someone picking up a piece of shattered glass,
afraid it might cut,
but too tender to leave it broken.
And in that moment,
Hosea is not just a husband,
he is a reflection,
a parable written in skin and bone,
a mirror showing us
the face of a God
who will buy back what belongs to Him,
no matter the cost.

He brings her home,
not as a servant,
not as someone to be punished,
but as his wife,
as someone worth loving,
even when the world said otherwise.
And this is what he tells her:
"You must dwell as mine for many days.
You shall not play the whore,
or belong to another man.
So will I also be to you."

There is no vengeance in his voice,
only the promise of something deeper
than desire,
something more faithful
than mere obligation.
He is asking for her heart,
for her presence,
for her to stay,
not out of duty,
but because love that is true
requires proximity.
It asks us to be near,
to be still,
to stop running long enough
to realize that home is not just a place,
but a person.

And this—
this is where the story stops being about Hosea and
Gomer,
and becomes about us.
Because we are Gomer,
standing on the auction blocks of our own making,
chasing lovers that leave us empty,
building altars to gods that don't know our names.
We are the ones who sell our souls
for the promise of something shiny,
something fleeting,
something that feels like love
but is really just lust
wearing a mask.

And yet,
God—

He walks into the marketplace,
sees us standing there,
broken and bruised,
and says,
"I will buy you back."
Not with silver,
not with barley,
but with blood.
With His own heart,
poured out like wine,
spilled like a promise
that cannot be taken back.

"For the children of Israel
shall dwell many days without king or prince,
without sacrifice or pillar,
without ephod or household gods."
There will be a season of wandering,
a time when we forget
the sound of God's voice
and the weight of His name on our lips.
But even in the silence,
even in the distance,
God waits.
He waits like Hosea waited—
not with bitterness,
but with a love that is as patient
as it is persistent.

"Afterward the children of Israel shall return
and seek the Lord their God,
and David their king,
and they shall come in fear to the Lord
and to His goodness in the latter days."

Because love, real love,
is always a return.
It is the journey back to the place
where we first belonged,
where we were always meant to be.
And God—
He is not just waiting for us,
He is coming for us,
running down the road with arms wide open,
ready to buy us back
again and again,
no matter how many times
we have sold ourselves
to things that could never hold us.

Hosea,
his heart heavy with the weight of it all,
now understands
that this is what love looks like.
It is not soft.
It is not easy.
It is the kind of love
that breaks you
and rebuilds you,
the kind of love
that says,
"I will not leave you
even when you leave Me."
The kind of love
that walks into the darkest places
and brings you home.

So here we are,
standing in the marketplace,

worn and weary,
wondering if we are worth it.
And God—
He steps forward,
looks us in the eyes,
and says,
"I will buy you back."

Truth Laid Bare

God's voice breaks the silence like thunder,
but it isn't the kind of thunder that comes with rain,
it's the kind that comes with a reckoning.
The courtroom is open,
and the earth is the witness,
the sky the jury.
God stands as both judge and plaintiff,
His heart heavy with the weight
of a covenant bruised by betrayal.

"Listen to the word of the Lord, O children of Israel,
for the Lord has a controversy
with the inhabitants of the land."
This is not a gentle conversation,
this is a confrontation,
a moment where truth,
sharp as glass,
is laid bare on the table
for everyone to see.

"There is no faithfulness or steadfast love,
and no knowledge of God in the land;
there is swearing, lying, murder,
stealing, and committing adultery;
they break all bounds,
and bloodshed follows bloodshed."
The list unfolds like a ledger,
one sin stacked on top of another,
until the weight of it crushes the very ground
beneath their feet.

The people,
they have forgotten
the sound of God's name.
They have replaced His voice
with idols made of stone,
with promises carved out of gold.
They swear by things that can't speak,
lie to themselves with every breath,
their hands stained with the evidence
of a love they betrayed long ago.

And God—
His heart is not angry,
it is aching.
His voice isn't a sword,
it's a sigh.
Because this isn't just about breaking laws,
this is about breaking hearts,
about a people who were supposed to be His
but have wandered so far
they can no longer recognize His face.

"Therefore the land mourns,
and all who dwell in it languish,
and also the beasts of the field
and the birds of the heavens,
and even the fish of the sea are taken away."
Creation itself is groaning,
as if the trees, the rivers, the soil
all know what the people have forgotten.
The earth mourns,
because it remembers what we don't—
that we were meant to walk with God,
to know His voice
like we know the sound of our own breath.

"Yet let no one contend,
and let none accuse,
for with you is my contention, O priest."
The priests,
the ones who were supposed to lead,
to stand in the gap between God and man,
have become just as lost,
just as blind.
They feed the people lies,
offer sacrifices that mean nothing,
their hands busy building altars
to gods that can't hear.

"My people are destroyed
for lack of knowledge;
because you have rejected knowledge,
I reject you from being a priest to me."
The knowledge of God
is not just information,
it is intimacy.

It is knowing Him like you know the rhythm
of your own heartbeat,
like you know the way the sky shifts from day to
night.
But Israel has traded that knowledge
for ignorance wrapped in arrogance,
and now they are paying the price.

The more the priests increased,
the more they sinned against Him;
they exchanged their glory
for something disgraceful,
fed on the sins of the people,
and made themselves fat
on the emptiness of false worship.
And God's anger burns,
not because He desires vengeance,
but because He desires relationship,
and they have torn it apart
piece by piece.

The people,
they are stubborn as a wild ox,
pulling away from the yoke,
refusing to be guided,
and God's hands,
though strong,
do not force.
He lets them go,
lets them wander,
even as His heart breaks
with every step they take away from Him.

"Though you play the whore, O Israel,
let not Judah become guilty."
He warns Judah,
the sister nation,
not to follow in Israel's footsteps,
not to fall into the same trap
of forgetting the One
who brought them out of the wilderness,
who gave them a land of their own.
He warns them
because He knows how easy it is
to let the heart stray,
to let the eyes wander
toward things that glitter
but are not gold.

"Do not go to Gilgal,
do not go up to Beth-aven,
and do not swear, 'As the Lord lives.'"
These places, once sacred,
have become tainted,
polluted with idolatry.
The people use God's name
like it's a tool,
like it's something they can manipulate
for their own desires,
but they have forgotten
that His name is holy,
that His name is a promise
that cannot be broken.

And then God says it,
the line that cuts through the noise,
that pierces the heart:

"Like a stubborn heifer,
Israel is stubborn;
can the Lord now feed them
like a lamb in a broad pasture?"
God is ready to feed them,
to care for them,
to lead them back to safety,
but they refuse.
They would rather wander in the wilderness
than rest in the green pastures
He has prepared for them.

"Ephraim is joined to idols;
leave him alone."
God's voice is resigned,
not because He has given up,
but because He knows
that sometimes,
the only way to teach someone
is to let them walk into the consequences
of their own choices.
Ephraim,
the largest tribe of Israel,
is so deeply entwined with idols
that it has become part of their identity,
and God lets them go,
even as His heart longs for them to return.

"When their drink is gone,
they give themselves to whoring;
their rulers dearly love shame."
The people have numbed themselves,
filled their emptiness with wine,
with fleeting pleasures,

but when the bottle is empty
and the laughter fades,
they are left with nothing but shame,
with the cold realization
that they have traded eternal joy
for temporary satisfaction.

A wind has wrapped them in its wings,
and they shall be ashamed
because of their sacrifices.
Like leaves caught in a storm,
they are tossed and turned,
pulled in every direction,
and when the storm is over,
they will see
that the altars they built,
the sacrifices they made,
were all for nothing.

And yet,
even in this moment of judgment,
there is the quiet, persistent hope
that they will return.
That they will remember the sound
of God's voice calling them by name,
that they will turn back
and find that He has been waiting
all along.
Because the story of Hosea
is not just about judgment,
it's about love.
A love that is fierce,
a love that is relentless,
a love that says,

"I will not give up on you,
even when you have given up on yourself."

And so,
the chapter ends,
not with a finality,
but with a pause,
a breath held in anticipation
of what could be,
if only they would return.

Heartbreak and Justice

The word of the Lord hits the ground
like a gavel, heavy and sharp.
And this time,
there's no space for hesitation,
no time for excuses.
It is judgment day,
and God speaks with the authority
of a father who has watched his children
run headlong into disaster.
This is not anger.
This is heartbreak wrapped in justice,
a declaration that the time for pleading
has passed.

"Hear this, O priests!
Pay attention, O house of Israel!
Give ear, O house of the king!
For the judgment is for you."
The leaders,
those who were supposed to guide,

who should have led with wisdom
and hands that healed,
they have failed.
They have become the blind
leading the blind,
walking the people straight into the mouth
of destruction.

"You have been a snare at Mizpah,
and a net spread upon Tabor."
The places that should have been holy,
that should have been sanctuaries,
have become traps,
snares set by those
who were supposed to protect.
And God's voice trembles,
not with anger,
but with the weight of it all,
with the knowledge that His people
have become prey
in a world of predators.

"The revolters have gone deep into slaughter,
but I will discipline all of them."
Revolt has become their language,
rebellion their mother tongue.
And though the slaughter is deep,
though their sin is like a canyon
carved by years of defiance,
God's discipline is not destruction.
It is correction.
It is the hand that pulls them back
from the edge,
even when they don't want to be saved.

"I know Ephraim,
and Israel is not hidden from me."
There is no hiding from the eyes of God.
He knows Ephraim's every secret,
Israel's every sin,
as intimately as a mother knows
the lines of her child's face.
And this knowledge—
it is not cold,
it is not clinical.
It is the kind of knowing
that breaks the heart,
because to know someone this deeply
is to love them,
and to love them
is to feel the full weight of their betrayal.

"For now, O Ephraim,
you have played the whore;
Israel is defiled."
They have turned to other lovers,
given their hearts to gods
that do not breathe,
to idols that cannot hold them.
And in the process,
they have defiled themselves,
covered themselves in the ashes
of their own destruction.
But even in this,
even in the midst of their whoring,
God sees them.
He knows them.
He has not turned His face away.

"Their deeds do not permit them
to return to their God,
for the spirit of whoredom is within them,
and they know not the Lord."
It is their actions that hold them captive,
their own choices that have chained them.
The spirit of whoredom—
it is not just about lust,
it's about the relentless pursuit
of anything that isn't God,
about the way they have filled themselves
with everything but Him.
And in doing so,
they have forgotten His name,
forgotten the sound of His voice
calling them home.

"The pride of Israel testifies to his face;
Israel and Ephraim shall stumble in their guilt;
Judah also shall stumble with them."
Pride has become a mirror
held up to their faces,
and what they see is their own downfall.
They stumble,
not because the path is unclear,
but because their eyes are closed,
their hearts too swollen with arrogance
to recognize the danger
that surrounds them.

"With their flocks and herds,
they shall go to seek the Lord,
but they will not find him;
he has withdrawn from them."

They come with offerings,
with sacrifices that mean nothing,
because their hearts are still far away.
They bring their flocks and herds,
thinking they can buy back
the favour of the God they have forsaken.
But God—
He has withdrawn.
Not out of spite,
but out of grief,
out of the deep sorrow
that comes from being constantly rejected
by the ones you love most.

"They have dealt faithlessly with the Lord,
for they have borne alien children."
Their faithlessness has led them
to birth something foreign,
something that does not belong to God.
The fruit of their rebellion
is not righteousness,
it is a generation that knows nothing
of the covenant,
a generation that has been raised
on the milk of idolatry.

Now the new moon
shall devour them with their fields.
Even the cycles of time
turn against them,
the new moon,
once a symbol of renewal,
now becomes a harbinger of their destruction.
The land itself rises up

to swallow them whole,
as if creation has grown tired
of their defiance.

"Blow the horn in Gibeah,
the trumpet in Ramah.
Sound the alarm at Beth-aven;
we follow you, O Benjamin!"
The call to arms echoes across the land,
a warning shot fired into the air.
The time for repentance is slipping away,
and the sound of the trumpet
is both a call to battle
and a lament for what is about to be lost.

"Ephraim shall become a desolation
in the day of punishment;
among the tribes of Israel
I make known what is sure."
God's judgment is not a possibility,
it is a certainty.
Ephraim, the once-proud tribe,
will become a wasteland,
a barren reminder
of what happens when pride
takes the place of humility.

The princes of Judah
have become like those
who move the landmark;
upon them I will pour out my wrath
like water.
The leaders have shifted the boundaries,
moved the markers of truth,

and in doing so,
they have led the people astray.
But God's wrath is not a wildfire;
it is like water,
flooding the land,
erasing the lines they have drawn,
restoring what they tried to destroy.

"Ephraim is oppressed,
crushed in judgment,
because he was determined
to go after filth."
This is the consequence
of chasing after filth,
of choosing the mud
when God offers the stars.
Ephraim is crushed,
not because God desires destruction,
but because their own choices
have led them to this place.

"But I am like a moth to Ephraim,
and like dry rot to the house of Judah."
God's presence is no longer a shelter,
it is a slow decay,
a moth eating away
at the fabric of their lives,
a rot that spreads through the bones
of their nation.
It is not sudden,
but it is certain,
and it is a consequence
of their refusal to return.

"When Ephraim saw his sickness,
and Judah his wound,
then Ephraim went to Assyria,
and sent to the great king.
But he is not able to cure you
or heal your wound."
They seek help from foreign kings,
from nations that cannot save them,
thinking that alliances will mend
what only God can heal.
But the king of Assyria
cannot bind their wounds,
cannot touch the sickness
that runs deep in their souls.

"For I will be like a lion to Ephraim,
and like a young lion to the house of Judah.
I, even I, will tear and go away;
I will carry off, and no one shall rescue."
God becomes the lion,
not in anger,
but in necessary judgment.
He tears,
not to destroy,
but to wake them up,
to remind them that there are consequences
for choosing other gods,
for turning their backs
on the One who carried them.

"I will return again to my place,
until they acknowledge their guilt
and seek my face,
and in their distress

earnestly seek me."
This is not abandonment.
This is love waiting on the edge of its seat,
waiting for the prodigal to come home.
God withdraws,
not out of spite,
but out of a longing for them to recognize
what they have lost,
to feel the emptiness of their choices,
to realize that the only way out
is to return.

And in their distress,
when the weight of their sin
finally breaks them,
they will look up,
they will seek His face,
and they will find
that He was waiting
all along.

A Cry to Return

It begins with a call,
a whisper in the wilderness,
a plea that's been buried in the dirt,
waiting to rise.
"Come, let us return to the Lord,"
because running away has left us limping,
and our legs are too tired to keep running
from a love that has never stopped chasing.

He has torn us,
but it is only to heal.
He has struck us down,
but His hands have always been surgeons,
cutting away what is killing us
so we can breathe again.

"After two days, He will revive us;
on the third day, He will raise us up,
that we may live before Him."

There is something about this love
that always leans toward resurrection,
always bends toward breathing life
into dead places,
as if God keeps seeds in His pockets,
ready to plant something beautiful
in every grave we dig for ourselves.

Let us press on to know the Lord.
Let us press in, lean forward,
because His coming is as sure as the dawn,
as certain as the sun lifting itself over the horizon
after the darkest night.
He will come to us like rain—
not the kind that floods,
but the kind that makes things grow.
He will be like showers on a parched land,
like water on the roots of a tree
that hasn't felt rain in years.

But then, God speaks—
and His voice is not thunder,
it is not fire,
it is the sound of someone
whose heart has been broken too many times.

"What shall I do with you, O Ephraim?
What shall I do with you, O Judah?"
It's the kind of question
that echoes in a parent's throat
when they've watched their child
fall into the same mistakes,
over and over again,
even after they've been warned,

even after they've been shown
another way.

Your love is like a morning cloud,
like the dew that goes away early.
It's fleeting,
it's temporary.
You say the right things,
you make promises with a silver tongue,
but when the sun comes up,
your devotion evaporates
like mist in the heat of the day.

So I have hewn them by the prophets,
I have slain them by the words of my mouth,
and my judgment goes forth as the light.
God's words have always been chisels,
cutting away the excess,
the lies,
the falsehoods we cling to,
until all that's left is truth—
sharp, shining,
undeniable in the light of His judgment.

But here's the thing:
"I desire steadfast love, not sacrifice,
the knowledge of God rather than burnt offerings."
He doesn't want empty rituals.
He doesn't want sacrifices made
with hearts that are a thousand miles away.
He wants love—
the kind that doesn't flicker out
when the morning comes.
He wants us to know Him,

to really know Him,
like the way we know the rhythm
of our own breathing,
like the way we know the sound
of our own name.

But like Adam,
they transgressed the covenant;
there they dealt faithlessly with me.
It's an old story,
one that repeats itself like a sad song
stuck on replay.
Like Adam,
we turn away.
Like Adam,
we choose to believe the lie
that there's something better
outside of God's love,
something worth trading our birthright for.

Gilead is a city of evildoers,
tracked with blood.
The priests,
the ones who should have been shepherds,
have become wolves.
They lie in wait for others,
murder on their minds,
sin in their hands.
They commit villainy,
and the land is soaked with the evidence
of their crimes.

In the house of Israel,
I have seen a horrible thing;

Ephraim's whoredom is there,
Israel is defiled.
It's a wound that runs deep,
a sickness that spreads like wildfire
through the bones of a nation
that was meant to be holy,
set apart,
a reflection of God's glory.
But now,
the mirror is cracked,
the image distorted,
and all that's left is a shadow
of what could have been.

For you also, O Judah,
a harvest is appointed.
The time is coming,
the day is near.
Judgment is not just for Ephraim,
not just for Israel.
Judah, too, will feel the weight
of their choices,
will taste the bitterness
of the fruit they have sown.

But even in this,
there is hope—
because God's heart
is never just for punishment,
it's for restoration.
He tears,
but He also heals.
He strikes,
but He also binds up.

And maybe, just maybe,
we will finally turn around
and see that His hands
have always been open,
waiting to catch us
when we finally fall
into His love.

The Heat of Hidden Flames

It starts with the heart,
every sin, every stumble
begins in a place that no one sees.
I imagine God looking at us
like a doctor examining a patient,
like a surgeon tracing the lines of disease
that spread in silence.
And He says,
"Whenever I would heal Israel,
the iniquity of Ephraim is revealed,
and the evil deeds of Samaria."
It's all coming to light,
the secrets we thought we could bury,
the sins we swore no one would notice.
But God's light doesn't just illuminate—
it exposes.

"They deal falsely;
the thief breaks in,
and the bandits raid outside."

It's not just one thing,
it's everywhere,
it's everything.
The corruption is so deep,
so woven into the fabric of their lives
that it feels normal now,
like breathing in smoke
until you forget what clean air tastes like.

But even in this haze of deceit,
God says,
"they do not consider
that I remember all their evil."
Like a parent watching
their child sneak around,
God sees every move,
every lie.
He remembers,
not because He's holding a grudge,
but because He knows that memory
is where healing begins.
You can't mend what you refuse to face,
you can't heal what you pretend isn't broken.

"By their evil,
they make the king glad,
and the princes by their treachery."
They've gotten so comfortable
with their wrongs
that they've turned them into entertainment,
making the powerful laugh
with their betrayal,
turning sin into sport,

as if the weight of their choices
won't crush them in the end.

"They are all adulterers;
they are like a heated oven
whose baker ceases to stir the fire."
And this is the part
that hits the hardest.
God looks at their hearts
and sees an oven,
burning, boiling,
a heat that no one is tending,
no one watching as it rages.
It's desire untamed,
passion unchecked,
a flame that's devouring everything
in its path.

From the rising of the sun
to its setting,
the fire grows,
but no one tends to it.
They sleep through the night,
dreaming of their schemes,
plotting their next steps
as the fire inside consumes them.

"On the day of our king,
the princes became sick with the heat of wine;
he stretched out his hand with mockers."
Even the leaders,
the ones who should have been sober,
should have been vigilant,
are drowning themselves in excess,

in the heat of wine and laughter,
stretching out their hands to those
who mock the very God
they were meant to serve.

"For with hearts like an oven
they approach their intrigue;
all night their anger smoulders;
in the morning it blazes
like a flaming fire."
Their hearts,
their anger,
it's like an oven that never cools down,
an inferno that smoulders through the night
only to burst into flames
at the break of dawn.
And God watches,
heart heavy,
knowing that this kind of fire
doesn't just burn the wicked—
it burns the whole house down.

"They are all hot as an oven,
and they devour their rulers.
All their kings have fallen,
and none of them calls upon me."
The kings,
the ones who were supposed to lead,
to guide,
are consumed by the very fire
they've stoked.
One by one,
they fall,
and still,

no one calls out to God.
The silence is deafening,
the absence of prayer
more tragic than the fall itself.

"Ephraim mixes himself with the peoples;
Ephraim is a cake not turned."
Half-baked,
that's what they've become.
Stuck in the middle,
caught between what they know is right
and what the world offers.
They've mixed themselves
with people who do not know God,
who do not care for His ways,
and now they're stuck—
cooked on one side,
raw on the other,
unable to be whole.

"Strangers devour his strength,
and he knows it not."
They're losing their power,
their strength slipping away
like water through fingers,
and they don't even realize it.
It's the kind of loss
that's so slow,
so quiet,
that by the time they notice,
it's too late.
Their hair is turning grey,
but they don't see it,

don't see the signs of decay
creeping into their bones.

"The pride of Israel testifies to his face;
yet they do not return to the Lord their God,
nor seek him, for all this."
Pride—
it's always pride
that stands in the way.
It's the voice that says,
"I'm fine,"
when everything is falling apart.
It's the refusal to admit
that they need help,
that they need God.
And so,
they keep walking,
heads held high
as the ground crumbles beneath them.

"Ephraim is like a dove,
silly and without sense,
calling to Egypt,
going to Assyria."
They're like a bird
flitting from branch to branch,
not knowing where to land.
Instead of returning to God,
they turn to other nations,
to Egypt and Assyria,
thinking that political alliances
can save them,
thinking that their safety

lies in the hands of men
who don't even know their God.

"As they go,
I will spread over them my net;
I will bring them down like birds of the heavens;
I will discipline them
according to the report made to their congregation."
But God,
He's not letting them fly away.
He spreads His net,
not to crush,
but to catch.
Even in their rebellion,
He is still the God
who doesn't let go,
who disciplines
because He loves,
because He knows
that they are birds
who have forgotten how to find their way home.

"Woe to them,
for they have strayed from me!
Destruction to them,
for they have rebelled against me!"
It's not anger that fuels these words,
it's grief.
It's the sorrow of a Father
watching His children walk away,
knowing that the path they've chosen
leads only to destruction.
And yet,

He still calls out,
still beckons them to turn back.

"I would redeem them,
but they speak lies against me."
God's heart is still for redemption,
still for restoration.
But they've built walls of lies
between themselves and their salvation,
convinced themselves
that God is not enough,
that His love is too small
to cover the vastness of their sin.

"They do not cry to me from the heart,
but they wail upon their beds;
for grain and wine they gash themselves;
they rebel against me."
Their prayers are shallow,
their cries only rise
when they're in need of grain,
of wine.
It's not their hearts that cry out,
it's their hunger.
And even in their desperation,
they rebel,
choosing self-inflicted wounds
over surrender.

"Although I trained and strengthened their arms,
yet they devise evil against me."
God,
the one who taught them how to stand,
how to fight,

how to be strong,
now watches as they use the strength
He gave them
to plot against Him.
It's the ultimate betrayal,
a child turning against the very parent
who taught them how to walk.

"They return,
but not upward;
they are like a treacherous bow."
They come back,
but not to God.
They return to their own ways,
to their idols,
to their empty rituals.
They're like a bow
that looks ready to shoot,
but bends in the wrong direction,
missing the mark every time.

"Their princes shall fall by the sword
because of the insolence of their tongue.
This shall be their derision in the land of Egypt."
And so,
their leaders will fall,
their words coming back to cut them down.
Their pride,
their insolence,
will be their undoing,
and the very nations they trusted
will mock them in the end.

And God's heart,
still breaking,
still waiting,
whispers one more time—
"Come home."

.

The Trumpet Call of Consequences

Sound the trumpet!
The warning rings out like thunder
across a sky that's been silent for too long.
It cuts through the air,
sharp as regret,
piercing the spaces we've left untouched
by truth.
It's time to face what's coming,
the reckoning that we've ignored,
the harvest of all the seeds we sowed
without a second thought.

"The eagle is over the house of the Lord,"
circling,
a predator waiting for the moment to strike.
But this isn't just about enemies,
about borders being breached.
This is about a betrayal,
a people who have forgotten
who they are

and whose they are.
They have transgressed my covenant
and rebelled against my law.
It's not just the walls that are broken—
it's the promises,
the trust,
the connection that once held
this whole thing together.

They cry to me,
"My God, we—Israel—know you!"
But it's a lie dressed in sincerity,
a confession without repentance,
a claim made with lips
that have tasted too much deceit
to remember what honesty tastes like.
It's like telling someone
you love them
after you've already packed your bags,
one foot already out the door.

Israel has spurned the good;
the enemy shall pursue him.
This is the result of all those choices,
all those times they turned away
instead of turning back.
They pushed goodness aside
like it was too heavy to carry,
and now the consequences
are running faster than they can.

They made kings,
but not through me.
They set up princes,

but I knew it not.
They built thrones
on foundations of arrogance,
elevating men who knew nothing
of my heart.
They chose leaders who promised power,
but never peace,
who spoke of strength,
but not of surrender.
It was always about control,
about building a kingdom for themselves
while forgetting the kingdom I had given them.

With their silver and gold
they made idols
for their own destruction.
It's ironic, isn't it?
They poured their wealth,
their energy,
their time
into statues that couldn't breathe,
into gods that couldn't even lift their heads
to see their suffering.
They built their own destruction
with their own hands,
crafting the very chains
that would bind them.

"I have spurned your calf, O Samaria.
My anger burns against them."
That golden calf—
the symbol of rebellion,
of forgetfulness,
of faith placed in the wrong things.

It stands there,
a mockery of everything
they were supposed to be,
and God's anger flares
not out of vengeance,
but out of heartbreak.
How long will it be
till they are pure?

For it is from Israel;
a craftsman made it;
it is not God.
That calf,
that idol,
it's nothing but metal
bent into a shape they could see,
because they were too afraid
to trust what they couldn't.
And the truth is this:
that false god
will be broken to pieces,
shattered like all the illusions
they've built their lives on.

For they sow the wind,
and they shall reap the whirlwind.
This is the law of return,
the law of harvest.
You plant seeds of emptiness,
you water them with deceit,
and what you get in return
is a storm.
They thought they could sow nothing
and still get something in return,

but the whirlwind doesn't ask for permission
when it comes to collect.

The standing grain has no heads;
it shall yield no flour.
The crops they counted on,
the success they thought was waiting
at the end of their rebellion—
it's all empty,
all hollow.
Even if it were to yield,
strangers would devour it.
Even their victories,
if they come,
will be taken from them,
swallowed by those
they thought they could outmanoeuvre.

Israel is swallowed up;
already they are among the nations
as a useless vessel.
They thought blending in
would protect them,
thought that losing themselves
in the crowd
would make them invisible
to the consequences.
But now,
they are swallowed,
devoured by the very nations
they tried to imitate.
They've become a vessel
with no purpose,
drifting with no direction.

For they have gone up to Assyria,
a wild donkey wandering alone.
They've turned to foreign powers,
to alliances with enemies,
like a donkey wandering in the wilderness,
wild and untamed,
thinking it can find its own way.
But what they'll find is loneliness,
a deep isolation
that comes from chasing after things
that can never fill the void.

Ephraim has hired lovers.
They've paid for affection,
for protection,
for peace,
but these hired lovers
don't care about them.
They take what they can get
and leave when the price is too high.

Though they hire allies among the nations,
I will soon gather them up.
Even in their wandering,
even in their rebellion,
God's plan is still in motion,
His hands still at work.
He will gather them,
not to scatter,
but to save.
Even as they chase after false lovers,
God waits for the moment
when they'll remember
what real love feels like.

And the king and princes
shall soon writhe
because of the tribute.
The leaders,
the ones who thought
they could buy safety,
will find themselves squirming
under the weight of their own deals,
the price they've paid
too heavy to bear.

Because Ephraim has multiplied altars for sinning,
they have become to him altars for sinning.
They built altars,
so many altars,
thinking that more rituals
would cover their rebellion,
thinking that sacrifices
could make up for their disobedience.
But those altars became the very thing
that ensnared them,
turned into monuments
of their sin instead of sanctuaries of grace.

Were I to write for him my laws
by the ten thousands,
they would be regarded as a strange thing.
God's words,
His laws,
have become foreign to them,
like a language they once knew
but have forgotten.
Even if He gave them endless instructions,

they wouldn't recognize the voice
that's been calling them home all along.

As for my sacrificial offerings,
they sacrifice meat and eat it,
but the Lord does not accept them.
Their sacrifices are empty,
just meat on an altar,
because their hearts aren't in it.
The rituals,
the offerings,
they mean nothing
when the hands that offer them
are stained with rebellion.

Now He will remember their iniquity
and punish their sins;
they shall return to Egypt.
There comes a time
when the bill comes due,
when the consequences
can no longer be delayed.
God remembers,
not out of anger,
but out of justice.
And now,
the road leads back to Egypt,
back to the place of slavery
they thought they'd left behind.

For Israel has forgotten his Maker
and built palaces,
and Judah has multiplied fortified cities.
They've forgotten who made them,

forgotten the One
who formed them from dust,
who brought them out of nothing
and gave them everything.
Instead,
they built their own palaces,
fortified their own cities,
thinking that walls and wealth
could keep them safe.
But no wall can hold back judgment,
no palace can protect from the truth.

So I will send a fire upon his cities,
and it shall devour her strongholds.
The fire is coming,
not to destroy for destruction's sake,
but to consume what's been built
on falsehoods and lies.
The strongholds,
the fortresses they trusted in,
will burn,
because sometimes,
the only way to rebuild
is to let the old things
turn to ash.

The Sorrow of a Love Forgotten

Rejoice not, O Israel!
Do not sing songs in the streets,
do not let the laughter rise
from your lips like smoke
that clouds the truth.
For you've sold yourself
for the harvest,
you've traded love for the luxury
of grain,
and now,
even the fields are cursed,
even the soil knows
what it feels like to be betrayed.
You have played the whore,
forsaking your God.

The threshing floor,
the winepress,
will not feed you anymore.
The grain that once filled your hands

will slip through your fingers
like sand,
and the wine you've longed for
will dry up before it even reaches your lips.
Because abundance can't grow
in the soil of sin,
and the feast you built on lies
will soon turn into famine.

"They shall not remain in the land of the Lord."
This land that was supposed to be home,
a promise kept,
a gift wrapped in sunlight and soil—
it will no longer hold you.
You will be uprooted,
exiled from the very earth
that once whispered your name in the wind.
And Egypt,
yes Egypt,
the place you fled from in chains,
will be your refuge.
But there's no refuge in running back
to the very thing
that once enslaved you.

Assyria—
you'll eat unclean food there,
you'll taste the bitterness of captivity
on your tongue.
Because when you trade freedom for false gods,
you find yourself hungry in foreign lands,
longing for the bread of home,
but too far gone to taste it.

They shall not pour drink offerings of wine
to the Lord.
No more sacrifices,
no more altars built on empty promises.
Their offerings will be like bread
for mourners—
unclean,
unwanted.
It will not enter the house of the Lord,
for their hands are stained
with the blood of rebellion,
their hearts too far removed
from the God they once called Father.

What will you do
on the day of the appointed festival,
and on the day of the feast of the Lord?
When the celebrations come,
when the calendar calls you to rejoice,
what will you offer?
When the trumpet sounds,
will you remember
how to dance before the Lord,
or will you be too far away
to hear the music?

For behold,
they are going away from destruction,
but Egypt shall gather them,
Memphis shall bury them.
They flee,
but destruction follows like a shadow,
chasing them into the arms of Egypt,
into the graveyards of Memphis.

Their precious things of silver
shall be covered with nettles,
their tents overrun with thorns.
Everything they thought was valuable,
everything they built and bought and held onto—
it will be swallowed by weeds,
buried in the thorns
of neglect and judgment.

The days of punishment have come;
the days of recompense have arrived;
Israel shall know it.
It's not just a storm on the horizon,
it's here,
it's now.
The winds of consequence
are whipping through the streets,
and Israel,
you can no longer pretend
that it's not coming for you.
You will know it,
you will feel it,
you will face it.

The prophet is a fool;
the man of the spirit is mad,
because of your great iniquity
and great hatred.
You've turned truth into madness,
made prophets into lunatics
because their words don't fit
the narrative of comfort
you've been feeding yourself.
You laughed at the warnings,

called wisdom foolish,
and now the truth
comes like a hurricane
to tear down the lies
you built your life on.

The prophet is the watchman
of Ephraim with my God.
But snares are on all his ways,
and hatred in the house of his God.
The watchman,
the one who stood guard
with God's word on his lips—
he's been trapped,
caught in the snares of deceit,
mocked in the very house
that was supposed to be holy.
Hatred filled the pews,
and the sanctuary turned into a den of lies.

They have deeply corrupted themselves
as in the days of Gibeah.
There,
at Gibeah,
where sin was a sickness,
where the darkness of man's heart
was laid bare—
that's where you've returned.
History repeating itself
like a broken record
that never learned its lesson.
He will remember their iniquity;
He will punish their sins.
The time for forgetting is over,

the time for grace has run out.
Now,
judgment comes not as a warning,
but as a reality
you can't escape.

Like grapes in the wilderness,
I found Israel.
God's voice softens here,
a flicker of the tenderness
that still remains in His heart.
He remembers the first love,
the sweetness of finding Israel
like grapes in the wilderness,
a rare and precious thing
in a barren place.
Like the first fruit on the fig tree
in its first season,
I saw your fathers.
There was a time
when they were ripe,
when they were ready,
when the fruit of their faith
was something beautiful to behold.

But they came to Baal-peor
and consecrated themselves
to the thing of shame,
and became detestable
like the thing they loved.
They traded that sweetness
for shame,
for idols that couldn't breathe,
for gods that turned them

into something they were never meant to be.
They loved what was detestable,
and in doing so,
became detestable themselves.

Ephraim's glory
shall fly away like a bird—
no birth,
no pregnancy,
no conception.
The glory they once held,
the honour that once crowned them—
it will vanish,
slip through their hands like feathers
caught in the wind.
The future they hoped for,
the generations they dreamed of—
it will be cut off,
withered before it ever blooms.

Even if they bring up children,
I will bereave them
till none is left.
Woe to them
when I depart from them!
Even the children they raise,
the ones they place their hopes in—
they will be taken,
lost to the winds of judgment.
And what is more tragic
than a future that's been erased?

Ephraim,
as I have seen,

was like a young palm planted in a meadow,
but Ephraim must lead his children out to slaughter.
There was a time
when Ephraim was full of life,
like a young palm swaying in the breeze,
growing in a meadow of grace.
But now,
that life has been twisted,
turned into death,
and the children they lead
are walking straight into the jaws of destruction.

Give them, O Lord—
what will you give?
Give them a miscarrying womb
and dry breasts.
Even the blessings of birth
will turn into curses,
the wombs that should have carried life
will only carry sorrow.
The source of nourishment
will be dried up,
and hope will wither
before it ever takes root.

Every evil of theirs
is in Gilgal;
there I began to hate them.
Because of the wickedness of their deeds
I will drive them out of my house.
There, at Gilgal,
the place where they once found God,
the place of crossing over,
has now become the place of rejection.

God's house,
once a refuge,
has closed its doors to them,
and they are left outside
with nothing but their sins
to keep them company.

I will love them no more;
all their princes are rebels.
The love that once held them,
the grace that covered them—
it's been withdrawn.
Their leaders,
their princes,
have led them astray,
and now,
there's no one left to guide them back.

Ephraim is stricken;
their root is dried up;
they shall bear no fruit.
The tree has withered,
the roots dried and cracked,
no longer drawing life
from the soil.
And without roots,
there can be no fruit,
no harvest,
no future.

Even though they give birth,
I will put their beloved children to death.
It's a hard truth,
a bitter reality.

Even the children they cherish
will not be spared
from the judgment that's coming,
because the sins of the fathers
have laid a path of destruction
for their sons and daughters.

My God will reject them
because they have not listened to Him;
they shall be wanderers among the nations.
The final word,
the closing chapter of this tragedy—
rejection.
Not because God has stopped loving,
but because they have stopped listening,
stopped hearing the voice
that has been calling them home
for so long.
Now, they will wander,
lost among the nations,
a people without a home,
without a God to call their own.

.

The Cracked Soil of a Divided Heart

Israel is a luxuriant vine,
a vine once rich with fruit,
flourishing,
but that abundance became their downfall.
They stretched toward the sun,
but they twisted their branches
around idols,
their roots entangled in greed.
The more his fruit increased,
the more altars he built;
the richer his land became,
the more he adorned his pillars.
They couldn't see that their blessings
were a test,
that abundance was supposed to bring them
closer to the Giver,
but instead,
they worshipped the gift,
poured their love into stone
instead of into the hands of God.

Their heart is false;
now they must bear their guilt.
There's a fracture in the soil
of their soul,
a crack that runs deep,
dividing who they are
from who they were meant to be.
Their heart is split,
fickle,
faithless.
They've made promises with their lips,
but their actions betray them.
Now, they must bear their guilt—
the weight of all the words they never meant,
the vows they broke
as easily as clay shatters on the floor.

The Lord will break down their altars
and destroy their pillars.
Those monuments to their pride,
the stone towers they raised
to gods who never spoke back—
God will break them.
Every altar they built with unclean hands
will fall,
every pillar they adorned with their vanity
will crumble into dust.

For now they will say:
"We have no king,
for we do not fear the Lord;
and a king—what could he do for us?"
They'll realize,
but too late,

that they put their trust in kings
who couldn't save them,
leaders who couldn't lead.
Without fear of the Lord,
without a reverence for the One
who holds the universe together,
what could a king do?
A crown is useless
if the heart beneath it
doesn't bow to God.

They utter mere words;
with empty oaths they make covenants;
so judgment springs up
like poisonous weeds
in the furrows of the field.
Their words,
their promises—
they're like breath in the wind,
empty,
insincere,
floating away the moment they're spoken.
And from those empty oaths,
from those hollow covenants,
judgment grows
like weeds in a field,
poisonous and choking,
turning what could have been a harvest
into nothing but decay.

The inhabitants of Samaria tremble
for the calf of Beth-aven.
Its people mourn for it,
and so do its idolatrous priests—

those who rejoiced over it and over its glory—
for it has departed from them.
They'll mourn,
weep for the idol they lost,
grieve for the calf of Beth-aven,
as if it could ever have saved them.
The priests,
the ones who danced around false gods
with hearts full of pride—
they'll tremble now,
because the thing they worshipped
has vanished,
the glory they chased
has departed,
slipped through their hands
like dust.

The thing itself shall be carried to Assyria
as tribute to the great king.
Ephraim shall be put to shame,
and Israel shall be ashamed of his idol.
The calf they once adored
will be carried away,
nothing but a trophy of their defeat,
a tribute to the conqueror.
And the shame that once clung to their souls
will now be on display,
their idol paraded through foreign lands,
their pride turned into humiliation.

Samaria's king shall perish
like a twig on the face of the waters.
Their king,
the one they trusted to save them,

will break,
snap like a twig
floating helpless on the currents,
swept away by the tide
of their own destruction.

The high places of Aven,
the sin of Israel,
shall be destroyed.
Thorn and thistle shall grow up
on their altars,
and they shall say to the mountains,
"Cover us,"
and to the hills,
"Fall on us."
The places they once worshipped,
the altars they built with pride—
they'll be overrun with thorns,
choked by weeds.
The sin of Israel
will stand no more,
and when the weight of their judgment
becomes too heavy to bear,
they'll cry out to the mountains,
begging the earth to swallow them whole,
to cover their shame.

From the days of Gibeah,
you have sinned, O Israel;
there they have continued.
Gibeah—
that name echoes through history,
a place where sin was allowed to fester,
where darkness thrived.

And from those days,
you have sinned, Israel.
You never left Gibeah behind,
you carried its shadow with you,
let its sins grow roots
in your heart.

Shall not the war against the unjust
overtake them in Gibeah?
God will bring war,
judgment,
against the injustice that thrived in Gibeah.
The time for reckoning has come,
and the sins of the past
will no longer be ignored.

When I please,
I will discipline them,
and nations shall be gathered against them
when they are bound up
for their double iniquity.
God's hand is steady,
His discipline certain.
The nations will gather,
the consequences of their sins
will encircle them like chains.
For their double iniquity—
the sins they doubled down on,
the rebellion they refused to repent from—
they will be bound,
tied by the very cords
they wove with their own hands.

Ephraim was a trained calf
that loved to thresh,
and I spared her fair neck;
but I will put Ephraim to the yoke;
Judah must plow;
Jacob must harrow for himself.
Ephraim,
once free,
once blessed to thresh the grain
without burden,
will now be yoked,
tied to the weight of their rebellion.
Judah must plow,
Jacob must work the hard ground,
because the soil they've left untended
is full of thorns,
full of weeds,
and it will take labour,
it will take pain,
to turn it back into something fruitful again.

Sow for yourselves righteousness;
reap steadfast love;
break up your fallow ground,
for it is the time to seek the Lord,
that He may come
and rain righteousness upon you.
There's still hope,
even in the wreckage,
even in the ruins.
Sow righteousness,
plant seeds of goodness in the soil of your heart,
and you'll reap love—
a love that's steadfast,

unmoving.
But first,
you must break up your fallow ground,
the hard earth that's grown cold,
the places in your soul
you've left untouched,
unbroken.
It's time to seek the Lord,
to turn back before the rains of judgment fall,
to ask for the rain of righteousness instead,
to water your weary heart
with His grace.

You have ploughed iniquity;
you have reaped injustice;
you have eaten the fruit of lies.
But here's the truth, Israel:
you've been planting the wrong seeds.
You've ploughed iniquity,
and now,
you're reaping a harvest of injustice.
The fruit you've been feasting on
is made of lies,
bitter and empty,
and now your stomach aches
from all the deceit you've swallowed.

Because you have trusted in your own way
and in the multitude of your warriors,
the tumult of war shall arise among your people,
and all your fortresses shall be destroyed.
You trusted in yourself,
in your strength,
in the power of your warriors.

You built walls,
fortresses of pride,
thinking they would keep you safe.
But war is coming,
and those walls will fall,
those fortresses will crumble,
and you'll find yourself defenceless
in the face of the storm.

As Shalman destroyed Beth-arbel
on the day of battle,
mothers were dashed in pieces
with their children.
The brutality of it—
the violence that you thought
was far away—
it's coming to your doorstep.
Beth-arbel,
its name stained with blood,
its streets marked with the cries of mothers
and the silence of children.
That day of battle
will come to you,
and you will feel the weight
of your own choices.

Thus it shall be done to you, O Bethel,
because of your great evil.
At dawn,
the king of Israel
shall be utterly cut off.
Bethel,
the house of God,
now a house of rebellion—

you will taste the bitterness
of your own great evil.
And when the morning comes,
when the sun rises on your judgment,
your king,
the one you trusted in,
will be cut off,
gone like a shadow at dawn.

A Father's Heart a Rebel's Cry

When Israel was a child, I loved him,
and out of Egypt, I called my son.
You were small then,
your steps uncertain,
your hands barely able to grasp
the weight of the world.
But I carried you,
cradled you in the curve of My palm,
and when you cried out in Egypt,
I was the one who heard.
I called you out of chains,
out of darkness,
out of a history that wasn't meant to be yours.

But the more I called them,
the more they went away.
It was like chasing the wind,
reaching for a son
who kept slipping out of My arms,

running in the opposite direction.
The more I whispered,
the more you fled,
drawn to gods that didn't know your name,
to altars where love was nothing
but a shadow.

They kept sacrificing to the Baals
and burning offerings to idols.
I watched as you bent your knee
to statues made of stone,
offered your heart to idols
that couldn't breathe.
I stood there,
silent,
as you burned offerings to gods
who never gave you anything
but silence in return.

Yet it was I
who taught Ephraim to walk;
I took them up by their arms,
but they did not know
that I healed them.
Do you remember those first steps,
when your legs were wobbly
and the ground seemed too far away?
It was My hands
that held you steady,
that kept you from falling.
Every stumble,
every scraped knee—
I was there.
I was the one who lifted you up,

the one who bandaged the wounds
you didn't even know you had.

I led them with cords of kindness,
with the bands of love,
and I became to them
as one who eases the yoke
on their jaws,
and I bent down to them
and fed them.
It wasn't chains that held you close,
wasn't the weight of law or burden.
It was love—
pure,
simple,
a love that wrapped around you
like a father's embrace.
I bent down,
knelt in the dust beside you,
and when you were too weak to feed yourself,
I fed you,
held the bread of heaven
to your lips,
but you didn't recognize the taste.

They shall not return to the land of Egypt,
but Assyria shall be their king,
because they have refused to return to Me.
The path you're on
doesn't lead back to Egypt,
but to Assyria,
to another land of chains,
another land of exile.
You turned your face away from Me,

and now the winds of consequence
are carrying you away.

The sword shall rage against their cities,
consume the bars of their gates,
and devour them
because of their own counsels.
You built walls around yourselves,
fortresses of pride,
but the sword is coming,
cutting through the defences you thought
would keep you safe.
The advice you followed—
it will be your undoing,
and the gates of your cities
will burn with the fire of your own rebellion.

My people are bent on turning away from Me,
and though they call out to the Most High,
He shall not raise them up at all.
You're determined,
set in your ways,
bent on walking away,
even when your legs are tired,
even when the road leads nowhere.
You cry out in your distress,
but it's not Me you're calling—
it's just another plea
to save yourselves,
another cry for mercy
with no desire to repent.

How can I give you up, O Ephraim?
How can I hand you over, O Israel?

How can I make you like Admah?
How can I treat you like Zeboiim?
My heart recoils within Me;
My compassion grows warm and tender.
And here is the ache,
the tearing of a Father's heart.
How can I give you up?
How can I let you go,
let you fall like Admah,
be destroyed like Zeboiim?
My heart pulls back,
it recoils,
because even in your rebellion,
I still love you.
Even in your defiance,
My compassion burns,
tender and unyielding.

I will not execute My burning anger;
I will not again destroy Ephraim;
for I am God and not a man,
the Holy One in your midst,
and I will not come in wrath.
I could have destroyed you,
could have let the fire of My anger
consume every piece of your rebellion,
but I am not a man,
I am God—
and My mercy is bigger than your sin,
My love deeper than your defiance.
I will not come with wrath
because I choose to come with grace,
even when you don't deserve it.

They shall go after the Lord;
He will roar like a lion;
when He roars,
His children shall come trembling
from the west.
There will come a day
when you will follow again,
when the sound of My voice
will reach you like thunder,
and you will come trembling,
broken,
but willing.
You will know the sound of your Father's roar,
and it will draw you back
from the places you've wandered.

They shall come trembling like birds from Egypt,
and like doves from the land of Assyria,
and I will return them to their homes,
declares the Lord.
You'll come back,
like birds set free,
like doves flying from the hands of oppression.
From Egypt,
from Assyria,
from the lands of exile and sorrow—
you'll return,
and I will be there,
waiting,
ready to bring you home.

Ephraim has surrounded Me with lies,
and the house of Israel with deceit,
but Judah still walks with God

and is faithful to the Holy One.
Even now,
even after all this,
you surround Me with lies,
deception wrapped around your hearts.
You say My name with your lips,
but your hearts are far from Me.
And yet,
there's still a flicker of faith,
a remnant of truth,
in Judah—
a people still walking with God,
still holding onto the thread of faithfulness
that ties them to the Holy One.

And here we stand,
a Father who will not give up,
a people who cannot see the love
that chases them down,
that carries them home
even when they keep running.
I am the Father,
the one who lifts you when you fall,
the one who calls you out of exile,
the one who waits,
arms wide,
heart open,
no matter how many times
you turn away.

The Wind and The Wrestle

Ephraim feeds on the wind
and pursues the east wind all day long.
You're chasing nothing,
hollow gusts that leave you breathless,
your hands wide open,
grasping at air.
You think you're moving forward,
but you're running in circles,
pursuing an east wind that offers nothing
but emptiness.
Each step you take
leaves you more lost than before,
further from the heart
that's been calling you home.

They multiply falsehood and violence;
they make a covenant with Assyria,
and oil is carried to Egypt.
You stack lies on top of lies,

weave violence into your daily bread.
You've made treaties with the world,
shaking hands with nations
that have no love for your God,
sending oil to Egypt
as if they could save you.
You keep trying to buy peace,
but you can't see that you're selling your soul.

The Lord has an indictment against Judah
and will punish Jacob
according to his ways;
He will repay him according to his deeds.
The scales of justice
are tipped with your own actions,
and the weight of your choices
presses heavy on the balance.
God isn't blind to the steps you've taken,
to the ways you've wandered.
The reckoning is coming,
and it won't be because He is cruel,
but because you've walked so far
into the wilderness of your own making.

In the womb,
he took his brother by the heel,
and in his manhood,
he strove with God.
Jacob—
you've always been wrestling,
even before you could speak,
even in the womb,
you grabbed your brother's heel,
fought for something

that was never yours to take.
And when you grew,
your fight wasn't with man anymore—
it was with God.
You wrestled with divinity,
grappled with the very hands
that shaped you.

He strove with the angel and prevailed;
he wept and sought his favour.
Jacob—
the one who wrestled until dawn,
the one who wouldn't let go
until the blessing was his.
But what they don't tell you
is how he wept,
how the fight was as much tears as fists,
as much surrender as it was strength.
He sought favour,
not through violence,
but through a heart that knew it needed more.

He met God at Bethel,
and there God spoke with us—
the Lord,
the God of hosts,
the Lord is His memorial name.
That was the moment,
the place where heaven touched earth,
where God spoke to a man
who had spent his whole life
running and wrestling.
And that's the name we carry,
the name of the God

who met Jacob in his brokenness,
who meets us still
in the places we least expect.

So you,
by the help of your God, return,
hold fast to love and justice,
and wait continually for your God.
Here's the invitation,
the challenge whispered through the ages:
Return.
It's not too late.
By the help of your God—
because you can't do this alone—
hold fast to love,
clasp justice tight in your hands
like a lifeline.
And wait,
wait for the God who has never abandoned you,
even when you abandoned Him.

A merchant,
in whose hands are false balances,
he loves to oppress.
You think you've gained much,
counting coins with crooked scales,
filling your pockets
with the weight of dishonesty.
But the wealth you love so much
has turned to chains around your soul.
You've become a merchant of deceit,
an oppressor dressed in robes of gold,
and the scales you use
will tip against you in the end.

Ephraim has said,
"Ah, but I am rich;
I have found wealth for myself;
in all my labours
they cannot find in me iniquity or sin."
You boast about your riches,
about the empires you've built
with your own hands.
You look around and say,
"I've earned this.
I am blameless.
No one can accuse me of wrong."
But your wealth is a mask,
a false armour,
and beneath it,
your heart is crumbling.

I am the Lord your God
from the land of Egypt;
I will again make you dwell in tents,
as in the days of the appointed feast.
Don't you remember,
Israel?
It was I who brought you out of Egypt,
who led you through the wilderness,
who gave you shelter in tents
when you had nothing but dust.
And now,
you've forgotten what it means
to rely on Me.
I'll strip it all away,
bring you back to the tents
where your heart can remember
what it's like to trust again.

I spoke to the prophets;
it was I who multiplied visions,
and through the prophets gave parables.
I have spoken in every way I could,
through visions that burned in the hearts of men,
through parables that sang truth
beneath the surface of words.
I've sent prophets to remind you,
to call you back,
but still, you closed your ears,
still, you turned your face away.

If there is iniquity in Gilead,
they shall surely come to nothing;
in Gilgal they sacrifice bulls;
their altars also are like stone heaps
on the furrows of the field.
Gilead—
once a place of healing,
now a land filled with iniquity.
And Gilgal,
where you've sacrificed bulls on altars,
your offerings piled high
like stones scattered in a field,
meaningless and cold.
The sacrifices you bring
are nothing but empty gestures,
your altars crumbling
beneath the weight of your own hypocrisy.

Jacob fled to the land of Aram;
there Israel served for a wife,
and for a wife he guarded sheep.
Remember Jacob,

how he fled,
how he served seven years for love,
how he guarded sheep
with nothing but his heart
and a promise.
Even he,
in all his wrestling,
knew what it meant to work for something pure,
to hold onto hope
in the midst of labour.

By a prophet
the Lord brought Israel up from Egypt,
and by a prophet
he was guarded.
It was by the voice of a prophet
that you were saved,
Israel.
It wasn't by your own strength,
not by your own wisdom.
You were guarded,
protected by a word that wasn't your own,
guided by a truth
that came from heaven.

Ephraim has given bitter provocation;
so his Lord will leave his bloodguilt on him
and will repay him for his disgraceful deeds.
But now, Ephraim,
you've pushed too far,
your heart full of bitterness
and provocation.
The Lord won't overlook it,
won't turn His face away from the bloodguilt

you've carried.
The scales will balance,
and the weight of your deeds
will fall back on you.
There's a cost to all the choices you've made,
and now the time has come
to pay the price.

The Echo of Kings and Dust

When Ephraim spoke,
there was trembling;
he was exalted in Israel,
but he incurred guilt through Baal and died.
Ephraim—
there was a time your voice held power,
a time when your words carried weight
and the nation trembled at your name.
You were exalted,
a king among kings,
but somewhere between glory and greed,
you turned away,
bowed down to Baal,
and in that bow, you broke.
In that moment,
your life was forfeit,
your heart was buried under the weight of idols.

And now they sin more and more,
and make for themselves metal images,
idols skilfully made of their silver,
all of them the work of craftsmen.
You didn't stop with one mistake,
didn't turn back after the first stumble.
No, you ran headlong into sin,
piling more and more onto your shoulders,
as if the weight would save you.
You made for yourself gods of silver,
idols crafted by human hands,
as if something man-made
could carry the soul of a nation.

It is said of them,
"Those who offer human sacrifice kiss calves!"
What kind of gods do you worship now,
Israel?
What kind of love leads you
to kiss the feet of a golden calf,
to offer human lives
on altars that don't even bleed?
Your lips press against cold metal,
and you call it faith,
but the only thing that grows from this soil
is death.

Therefore they shall be like the morning mist
or like the dew that goes early away,
like the chaff that swirls from the threshing floor
or like smoke from a window.
And here's the truth
you don't want to hear:
you're fading, Ephraim.

Your life is as fleeting
as morning mist,
as temporary as dew that disappears
before the sun is high.
You are chaff,
swirling in the wind,
scattered from the threshing floor
with no roots,
no anchor.
You are smoke rising from a window—
visible for a moment,
but soon lost in the sky.

But I am the Lord your God
from the land of Egypt;
you know no God but Me,
and besides Me there is no saviour.
Remember Me?
I was the one who brought you up
from Egypt,
the one who called your name
before you even knew who you were.
There is no other God,
no other saviour,
no other voice that whispered to you
in the wilderness.
You've forgotten,
but I've never stopped remembering.

It was I who knew you in the wilderness,
in the land of drought;
but when they had grazed, they became full,
they were filled, and their heart was lifted up;
therefore they forgot Me.

In the wilderness,
when you were nothing but dust and bones,
I knew you.
I watched over you,
fed you when there was no food,
gave you water when the land was dry.
But when you were full,
when your stomachs swelled with the abundance I
provided,
your hearts swelled with pride,
and you forgot Me,
the God who gave you everything.

So I am to them like a lion;
like a leopard I will lurk beside the way.
I will fall upon them like a bear
robbed of her cubs;
I will tear open their breast,
and there I will devour them like a lion,
as a wild beast would rip them open.
I didn't want it to come to this,
but you've left Me no choice.
Like a lion,
I will pounce,
like a leopard,
I will wait in the shadows.
I will come upon you
with the fury of a bear
robbed of her cubs,
tearing open the breast of a nation
that has forgotten its mother.
You will be devoured,
your pride ripped apart,

your idols shattered in the jaws
of the wild.

He destroys you, O Israel,
for you are against Me, against your helper.
This destruction isn't from a foreign land,
it isn't the hand of an enemy king.
No, Israel,
you're destroying yourself.
You've turned against your only Helper,
the one who held out His hand,
and in rejecting Me,
you've brought ruin to your own house.

Where now is your king,
to save you in all your cities?
Where are all your rulers—
those of whom you said,
"Give me a king and princes"?
You wanted kings,
remember?
You cried out for rulers,
for princes to govern you,
and I gave them to you.
But where are they now,
in your time of need?
Where is the king
who will save you from the storm
that's coming for your soul?

I gave you a king in My anger,
and I took him away in My wrath.
You wanted power,
so I gave it to you,

gave you a king in My anger,
knowing full well
he would lead you to ruin.
And now,
in My wrath,
I will take him away,
strip you of the very thing
you thought would save you.

The iniquity of Ephraim is bound up;
his sin is kept in store.
The pangs of childbirth come for him,
but he is an unwise son,
for at the right time
he does not present himself
at the opening of the womb.
Your sins are piled up,
stored in the treasury of your own rebellion.
And now,
like a woman in labour,
the pangs are coming for you.
But you're an unwise son,
Ephraim,
refusing to be born,
refusing to come forth
even when the time is right.
You've stayed in the womb too long,
and the birth you've delayed
will only bring more pain.

Shall I ransom them from the power of Sheol?
Shall I redeem them from Death?
O Death, where are your plagues?
O Sheol, where is your sting?

Compassion is hidden from My eyes.
You think you can escape,
that death won't touch you,
that Sheol's grip won't find your soul.
But where is your ransom now?
Where is the price that will save you
from the plagues of death?
I won't hold back this time.
Compassion has turned its face,
and judgment is what's left.

Though he may flourish among his brothers,
the east wind,
the wind of the Lord,
shall come,
rising from the wilderness,
and his fountain shall dry up;
his spring shall be parched;
it shall strip his treasury
of every precious thing.
You've flourished for a while,
grown fat on the blessings
that weren't yours to keep.
But the east wind is coming,
the wind of the Lord
rising from the wilderness,
and when it blows,
your fountains will run dry,
your springs will be parched.
The treasures you've stored up—
they will be stripped away,
every precious thing lost to the wind.

Samaria shall bear her guilt,
because she has rebelled against her God;
they shall fall by the sword;
their little ones shall be dashed in pieces,
and their pregnant women ripped open.
Samaria,
your guilt is heavy,
a burden you can't bear alone.
You've rebelled against your God,
and now the sword is at your gates.
The cruelty you showed
will be turned back on you—
innocent lives shattered,
the future ripped apart
before it can even breathe.

And this is how it ends,
Ephraim,
Israel—
not with the thunder of war,
but with the whisper of judgment,
with the howl of a wind
that takes everything
and leaves you standing
in the dust of your own making.

A Return to Love

Return, O Israel, to the Lord your God,
for you have stumbled because of your iniquity.
It starts with a whisper,
a gentle nudge in the dark,
the kind of invitation
that breaks the silence of the heart.
Return.
It's not a demand;
it's a longing wrapped in grace,
an outstretched hand
waiting to catch you
before you fall.

You've stumbled,
fallen into the depths of your own making,
but the ground beneath you
is not the end—
it's the beginning of a return,
a chance to shed the weight

of the choices that led you away,
to lift your eyes to the One
who has never turned away.

Take with you words
and return to the Lord;
say to Him,
"Take away all iniquity;
accept what is good,
and we will pay with bulls
the vows of our lips."
Bring your words—
not empty offerings,
but a heart that knows the weight of sin,
a voice that can name the darkness.
Take them back,
surrender them to the One
who knows your name,
who sees your struggle
and wants to take it all away.

You've made promises to false gods,
sacrificed to idols of your own making,
but this time,
let your vow be a plea for mercy,
a cry for the good
you've longed for
but could never find.
Come,
let your lips speak the truth,
and in that truth,
let your heart find rest.

Assyria shall not save us;
we will not ride on horses;
and we will say no more,
'Our God,'
to the work of our hands.
The Armor you've worn
is rusted,
and the horses you've ridden
are weary.
You thought power would save you,
thought strength could hold you steady,
but now you see
the emptiness in your own hands.
Assyria can't save you;
the clamour of horses will not bring peace.
It's time to lay down the weapons,
to stop leaning on the things
that crumble beneath your feet.

In the moment of surrender,
you will find your God—
the One who is not a distant king
but a close friend,
the one who meets you
in your trembling,
who sees the scars of your battles
and still calls you beloved.
The work of your hands has failed you,
but His hands are open,
waiting to fill the spaces
you've left empty.

I will heal their apostasy;
I will love them freely,

for my anger has turned from them.
There is a balm for your wounds,
a salve for your aching soul.
He will heal your brokenness
not with judgment,
but with love,
a love that knows no bounds,
that runs deeper than your rebellion.
He sees your wandering,
your wayward heart,
and He says,
"Come home.
Come back to the place
where love is real."

His anger—
it has turned away,
like a storm that passes,
leaving clear skies behind.
You don't have to live in fear,
waiting for the thunder to crack
and the rain to fall.
Instead, find shelter in His love,
let it wrap around you
like a warm embrace,
the kind that whispers,
"You are mine,
and I am yours."

They shall return and dwell beneath my shadow;
they shall flourish like the grain;
they shall blossom like the vine;
their fame shall be like the wine of Lebanon.
What a beautiful promise—

the return to the shadow
of the Almighty,
to dwell where the sun can't scorch,
to find rest beneath the arms
that hold the universe.
You'll flourish like grain,
rooted deep in rich soil,
standing tall in the warmth of love.

And as you return,
you'll blossom like a vine,
each tendril reaching for the sky,
each leaf a testament
to the grace that brings you back.
Your fame will not be found
in the things you've built,
but in the stories of redemption,
the tales of a heart restored,
like the wine of Lebanon—
sweet, rich,
full of life.

O Ephraim,
what have I to do with idols?
It is I who answer and look after you.
The question hangs in the air,
heavy with the weight of memory.
What have you to do with idols,
those hollow echoes of your heart's desire?
What have they done for you
except leave you empty?
Let them go—
let them fall
from the throne of your heart.

The One who answers,
who watches over you
with eyes that see,
is waiting in the silence,
longing for you to turn back.
He has not forgotten you,
even in your wandering.
His voice will always call,
echoing in the stillness,
reminding you of the love
that binds you to Him.

I am like an evergreen cypress;
from me comes your fruit.
In the depth of His being,
there is a promise—
a promise of life
that flows like rivers,
that springs up from the roots
of the evergreen.
You will find your fruit there,
the nourishment you've craved
but thought you lost.
It will grow from the depths of His love,
the kind of fruit that remains,
that holds the sweetness of grace.

Whoever is wise, let him understand these things;
whoever is discerning,
let him know them.
For the ways of the Lord are right,
and the upright walk in them,
but transgressors stumble in them.
This is wisdom,

the call to understand,
the invitation to discern the truth.
The ways of the Lord—
they are not burdensome,
but a path paved with love,
a road that leads home.

So listen,
Ephraim,
hear the call of the One
who waits for you,
who longs to embrace you,
who has never given up on your story.
The path may be winding,
the journey long,
but in each step,
there is grace,
and in each turn,
there is hope.
Return, O Israel,
for love is waiting,
and the heart of God
is open wide.

About The Author

Ruel Fordyce is an emerging poet whose work explores the depths of human emotion and the beauty of the natural world. Born in Trinidad and Tobago and raised in the city of Tunapuna, Ruel Fordyce discovered a love for words at a young age. Inspired by the works of Khalil Gibran, T.S. Elliot, C.S. Lewis and Rudy Francisco, they too began writing poetry as a means of self-expression and reflection.

His poetry has been praised for its vivid imagery, emotional resonance, and lyrical grace. In addition to writing, Ruel Fordyce is also passionate about the state of our environment, which often influence's his creative work. He has performed at poetry readings, captivating audiences with his powerful voice and heartfelt delivery.

Ruel Fordyce currently resides in Trinidad and Tobago, where he continues to write and inspire others with his poetry. When not writing, he enjoys spending time with his wife and two sons and, finding inspiration in the everyday moments that shape his poetic vision.

Made in the USA
Columbia, SC
17 October 2024